EACH ONE
A FURNACE

BOOKS BY TOLU OLORUNTOBA

The Junta of Happenstance

Manubrium

EACH ONE
A FURNACE

TOLU OLORUNTOBA

McClelland & Stewart

McClelland & Stewart and colophon are registered trademarks of Penguin Random House Canada Limited.

Published simultaneously in the United States of America.

Library and Archives Canada Cataloguing in Publication data is available upon request.

ISBN: 978-0-7710-5158-6
ebook ISBN: 978-0-7710-5159-3

Book design by Kate Sinclair
Cover art: (compass) Triff / Shutterstock Images

Typeset in LTC Goudy Old Style Pro by M&S, Toronto
Printed in Canada

McClelland & Stewart,
a division of Penguin Random House Canada Limited,
a Penguin Random House Company
www.penguinrandomhouse.ca

1 2 3 4 5   26 25 24 23 22

Penguin
Random House
McCLELLAND & STEWART

for those who can never be still

CONTENTS

II

III

I

CUTTHROAT

I'm a cutthroat
(as in, the one throatcut,
neck a red sash)
(they clutch their bags
and flinch).

Call the animal rent, that I trail in the forest of cured wood the city
is built on. The timber is still all here, of course: sheathed in concrete,

wearing the sky, buttoning my pinstripe jerkin. I must stay downwind,
still for the cunning buck. You can't tell the hunters, elevators of

notched presentations, scent-free in dawn's cloak, apart.
It is not sport that drives me to this,

but retirement from the hunt.
I cull the animal, rend it from its bedding.

Give me your thud against the brush, the door I open in your chest;
give me your antlers, enterprising, rising above the water.

ZEBRA

If / primeval forest,
made fire with cages of saws,

Then / men who unmade it
favored *an ideal beginner's bird,*
hardbill for flint,
white soutane streaked
with a soot rain,
cradling the eggs of other birds,
unwilling.

I wonder why it's the burning ones
we have nominated for our
suffering. Without hamstrings
you cannot stride forward,
only hobble through
fall rain, phrases
on your head
for arrival,
when
your remaining body heat can steam
your clothes as you lay down the word.
It's exhausting sometimes why
am I spokesman, agar
for dangerous tests
with spores blooming
from my mouth?
I want
the
id, subterranean life of this why.
I'm tired of these fire metaphors
but they want me to speak for
them through the flames and to,
when it's done, tell them
what the forest,
and its lit
hikers,
mean.

"During the trial, the judge, Mr. Justice Hinchcliffe—who at one point described Oluwale as "a dirty, filthy, violent vagrant"—directed the jury to find the defendants not guilty of manslaughter, perjury and assaults occasioning grievous bodily harm"

What we know:

1. The Black-rumped Waxbill, found in African grasslands,
   sometimes landing further afield,
   is a bird of Least Concern:
   not *a focus of species conservation.*
   They do not qualify as threatened.
2. The collective for a group of them, is a trembling;
3. A trembling:
   - David Oluwale in the hull of the SS *Temple Bar;*
   - The tailor's fabric in the wake of feet leaving the machine;
   - The voyage: Lagos to Hull, the stowaway's arrest after;
   - The year 1949; the age 19; the 20 years following:
   - The nightclub raid, the truncheon to the head; the
     hallucinations in jail;
   - The revenant beyond electroshocks; nights in the shut
     doorways of Leeds;
   - The sneer of the garment district;
   - The decade in mental hospitals
   - Another as target of Ellerker and Kitching;
     and the charge sheets of Leeds' finest
4. A trembling:
   - The last day, the chase by the riverbank;
   - Billy clubs Ellerker and Kitching in pursuit;
   - Oluwale, legs pumping by the River Aire;
   - Touchdown, splashback
5. A lack of trembling: rinsers of vagrants, collection from the river.

Serin bifascié, a French taxonomy
for two-faced birds named for the protean scrubs they nest in,
knowing they have no home.

Bioforming takes expeditions generations of refinement
in journeys to earth analogs. Terraforming will not always work;
not fast enough. Bend your biology to the harsh, evolve your own flesh.

Almost a hundred years have passed since we first
made our way down from the grasslands of the middle belt,
from farms into cities built around the British.

See how continental we be now,
watch our changes to tongue and passport hand,
our distrust of nationality, our allegiance to survival.

BILL-SWEEP

Was Nina feeling good
in the downdraft of feathers under
oracular horn sections,
within that song that wasn't of euphoria
but a burlesque of doom;
the swing, baritone of announcing trumpets
listing instances of molting from old world
of pine, and bird, and dragonfly, onto these streets
with a song to walk them? Earnest and brisk, we—
feathers and the bird they make,
blown, tarred skins rippling with us,
bent toward the gravity of deadlines,
the aerodynamic head tilt into the thing—
approach the early bird, down from flying high,
its beak in the subway wormhole.

Bramblings trundle in the smog
through the city's impassive fingers,
the brush bristles tangled with barbed phone signals.
Endangered, dispersed wide in massive flocks;
in paradox, in mossy camouflage, from the kestrel of obscurity,
commuting to and from a source of food,
a source of anything-but. Those bright
coats of diasporic winterbirds
have come for the beechmast of Europe, Asia, America.
And when others fall from the sky
in thousands, we'll already be gone.

BRONZE

Their last creation was this manikin.
From the last gasp of vanquishment,
the polyglot, the crafty, the shiny.

Advertising: open for business.
Not advertised: the song hid in the hollow,
Ovonramwen's ivory.

The fan: the ballistic shield.
The sheen: to reflect empire,
betray nothing.

Our first creation: a relief—
mettle for lost wax,
a superalloy, in potential space—

for the Africans coming.

I cut the placenta tree at the stem

the child's phantom other a weight
falling after

they'd asked me, do you want to
cut the cord?

blood spraying the shielding palm

do you want to cut away spices
pressed to newborn mouths?

pressing significances into progeny

do you want to cut down farms
on ritual supply routes?

honey for the sweetness some call joy;
good fortune from an alligator pepper's
pods;
palm oil, antidote of antidotes,
lubricant for the path;
the kola-nut spat to ward evil;
salt to season a life;
bitter kola to lengthen it;
and water, wey no get enemy

do you want to cut out night
burials of arcane afterbirths?

the knowing where a placenta is
planted,
the hiding it oneself;
away from jealous potion makers, or
its owner, forever:
a child's skeleton key.

do you want to cut off the
homeland?

ATTICUS FINCH

The obverse: to walk around in a man's skin,
you have to kill him or,
watchman, watch him skinned,
wear him for yourself.

How did finches soften while
I have only hardened? Faithless
elector, marred by violence, I descended
from flight, and exchanged my down
for bronzen mail. From the reptilian,
to the four-winged, wind-in-the-bones
nest builder, some undergo improvement.
Few scientists, anyway, dispute the dinosaur-
ian origin of birds. I, for one, accept that destiny,
surviving extinction, finding company at last,
as our passerine forms become chaos, then a spark,
then nothingness.

When I hear "Let's divide and conquer" in project management meetings, I wince and remember the British dicing knife.

The nurturing instinct, I see, is also a murderous instinct because parents, those notorious drivers of minivans, kill for their children. In this essay I will

demonstrate the Soylent Green operation of international trade, its battery cages of battery cages; my own family in ochre pajamas in the infinite condominium array.

Macroeconomics measures the methane doses of jailbirds, renovates old-growth forests into cul-de-sacs for its workers, installs Indigenous carbon filters in the earth,

and calibrates the valiums of domestic, and corporate life. But 200 years into the revolution of industry, the furnace is demanding more meat. The daily hunt in exercise

areas can therefore not be cruelty-free. We are, thankfully, the non-renewable scourge of this planet. That we are beasts, with useful beasts of our own in crates,

does not mean we do not harbour insurrection. Etheridge saw the globe for what it was: a penitentiary of cast iron meridians, and latitudes, the billionaires trying, in vain, to escape.

People invite poets for arson. If cowardice is our sigil
it is because we had no other choice. If our jumpsuits can burn
monoxide blue in cake ovens,

could we die, but preferably kill wardens, for our children? Cue the alarms, the barometer, the eschaton of our failing bodies.

PORTRAIT OF THE ARTIST AS GOULDIAN CHICK IN FREEFALL
FROM THE NEST

To say I lived a sheltered life also means I was sheltered
from safety, from hands that could have saved me from
the barbed crown of his nest. I was protected from leaving,
from other comforts but the soft between trampling talons.
I stabbed myself with the edge of escape. I have, by now,
fallen halfway across the planet. I will myself heavier,
farther away from the keening calling me back.

In the percussion of air currents, Àyán searches
the talking drums beside my eyes, with a tri-tonic song for me,
which I would bear, had I not slashed my skeins;
had I not drawn shades over my nictitating membranes;
had I repeated the chant prepared for me;
had I aimed upward instead,
the shotgun blast of my feathers.

Out of Niña's hand,
igneous plate, fickle water.

A seed goes in,
we grow, each generation
its own intermediate
of *insensibly graduated beaks.*

A song comes out
when we find
the food we can find,
the food says what our mouths
look like,
our mouths say what our
songs sound like,
our songs say
how, and if,
the hunting party finds us.

Our jaws have mouths
for each season
(*The greater number, jet black,
And brown*), each island of dispersion,
whatever quaver closest
to the key of demand.

I survived the old country, but at what cost?
Ibadan had fireflies but little light pollution,
and finches I had no names for on the telegraph
wires crossing the street, choreographing traffic,
resting from flight. I have not seen Orion's Belt
since I left, and seen finches only in the glass jars
of conservatories. But why did I nightmare being back
there, at the old job? What do I remember of binding
the infirmities of the body? What shall I do with
the hand-bowls of hope they present to me?

Touched little as a child except to be struck,
my partner cannot understand why I cannot endure
tickles. I flinch at the caress but finally understand:
I will not have control of my body taken
again. I thus understood the hardness of *Halo*'s
Master Chief, who took off neither armor, nor helmet.
His skin must have chafed under. Air would have raked
its lower incisors over any exposure
with the mentholated treachery of Robb.
He, perpetual veteran, would have longed for touch,
but been unable to suffer it.

Disorganized at the border of safety | danger,
I have never been able to lay down for love.
Forgive me. Don't touch me. Don't leave me.

Frantic, we pecked applications in the silt;
amputated limbic snares;
gave eyes in Hammurabic discipline
before we could
see gleams in the dirt and reach;
smelted sand
-banks into the Euphrates
with supplicant rubs
to become a monolith whittled,
and abstinent.

So when the last figures
worrying with picks,
the igneous trajectories within fell,
in sweat, or death,
we picked them gentle,
shielded with a rail-marked welcome,
the cars carrying shame farther inward,
through the bricolage around
the millennial glacier we clocked with
clues as we slipped in.

Today the old fort descends with the ice sheet,
meltwater combing the screes.
Weaverbirds have gone with the wheat
we are awoken from cryostasis by the crunch of absence,
the clay feet alluvial beside us on the plain
after martial marches downhill,
with the phantasm made seed,
the broken tree,
the new tools of refuge.

The nonpareil is the frightened bird.
Detainers love it for this reason,
above all others: the percussion, clap
against   cage walls when approached, slap
against   the roof when lights come on, burst
into panic, however cautious, or callous the tread;
the undark
arms of custody flailing clockwise; the turn
into the green of grove

of radium girls, who did as told once,
the *Perpetual Sunshine*, put to lips, as told, the nothing
they said about it exploding
their jaws. To bring light, *be* light,
air pockets eating bird bones;
to be shimmering, before knowing death was death,
the dust of work glowing ballrooms
after hours; to be steady, the ballast
of secret sarcomas holding
the truth of tools.

The Society, reliable once, remembers.
The concussion of cage rods on approach:
better that, than the experiments.

MASKED

I have nothing further to say of the allegations.
I forgive the secateurs, the jointed saboteurs.
We have naught, but the modicum of trims, now.
I have photos of us at 11, yours black-and-white;
the same pucker of shame,
the blind resolution I recognize;
eyelashes as grass curtains
for cataclysmic sparks.
Someone once wondered aloud
if we'd be alike in my old age.
Probably, but not if
I fire first, the visor and brush I'm made of.

We can afford corn, though.
Starch, binding our precarious diet,
mordant, slipknot of the belly's crochet.
I run my hands over new folds in the shower,
the orange weave hardening,
becoming Kevlar under my skin.
I know, from cadavers,
how tough this apron is to cut
away. Maybe now, knives will bounce off
if I'm stabbed.
But what of knives in the blood?

I think, vertiginous, of fat, and risk factors,
orange syrup swamping my pancreas,
clogging my arteries.

They say salads can sate the weaver,
unravel some thread.
We can afford corn, though.
Let us eat corn.

1: *Carbon-Based*

Everything is not right but
there aren't more people com-
busting in the streets.
Wasn't all that was needed
friction, some oxygen and willing bodies?

Those who watch the geopolitics
of effigies,
who see the stockpile
of bodies in flammable cities,
are concerned.

Everyone is waiting for something;
we are compacted, smokestacks walking,
cloth-bonded.

And those who distrust this calm beatific
shelter in place,
waiting for someone to ask—
wouldn't a little heat
be a good thing?

2: *Wars of Glass*

Some skies are hard
and will break your neck
if you fly into them,
and people will step around your body
on the sidewalk.

I have a broken neck
so I thought to tell you about
getting in these offices.

Amidst the forest of raised hands,
glassy fingers in low-visibility flight,
people tend to hurl themselves
forward.

All I know
are the wars of glass—
of striving birds and their causes,
and that to enter the only path,
the forest must gape itself at you
as you pick your way
through the barcode skyline.

Or *critically endangered.* https://www.iucnredlist.org/species/22720734
/126791352

Or *extinction probability.* https://ecos.fws.gov/docs/five_year_review
/doc4577.pdf

Or *scientific consensus.* https://www.itis.gov/servlet/SingleRpt
/SingleRpt?search_topic=TSN&search_value=554393#null

Or *historical range.* https://ecos.fws.gov/ecp0/profile/speciesProfile
?spcode=B00J

Or *every effort.* https://www.itis.gov/servlet/SingleRpt/SingleRpt
?search_topic=TSN&search_value=554393#null

Or *less than ten years.* https://birdsna.org/Species-Account/bna
/species/ou/introduction

Or *food resources.* https://www.hbw.com/species/ou-psittirostra
-psittacea

Or *predation by introduced mammals.* https://dlnr.hawaii.gov/wildlife
/files/2013/09/Fact-sheet-ou.pdf

Or *foraging areas.* https://birdsna.org/Species-Account/bna/species
/ou/introduction

Or *begging juveniles.* https://www.hbw.com/species/ou-psittirostra
-psittacea

Or *directly observed.* https://www.hbw.com/species/ou-psittirostra
-psittacea

Or *continuing decline in area, extent, and/or quality of habitat.*
https://www.iucnredlist.org/species/22720734/126791352

Or *warrant a change.* https://ecos.fws.gov/docs/five_year_review
/doc4577.pdf

Or *natural disasters.* https://dlnr.hawaii.gov/wildlife/files/2013/09
/Fact-sheet-ou.pdf

Or *remaining population.* http://datazone.birdlife.org/species/factsheet
/22720734

Or *seasonal outbreaks.* https://www.hbw.com/species/ou-psittirostra
-psittacea

Or *invasive species.* http://explorer.natureserve.org/servlet
/NatureServe?searchName=Psittirostra+psittacea

Or *habitat loss.* http://datazone.birdlife.org/species/factsheet
/22720734

Or *storms & flooding.* https://www.iucnredlist.org/species/22720734/
126791352

Or *lava flow.* https://en.wikipedia.org/wiki/ʻŌʻū

Or *great distances.* https://en.wikipedia.org/wiki/ʻŌʻū

Or *population trend.* http://datazone.birdlife.org/species/factsheet
/22720734

Or *generation length.* https://www.iucnredlist.org/species/22720734
/126791352

Or *continuing decline of mature individuals.* https://www.iucnredlist.org
/species/22720734/126791352

Or *evolutionary radiation.* https://www.britannica.com/animal
/Hawaiian-honeycreeper

Or *controlling the spread.* https://en.wikipedia.org/wiki/ʻŌʻū

Or *green back.* https://ecos.fws.gov/ecpo/profile/speciesProfile
?spcode=B00J

FIVE EYES

after Langston Hughes

I, too, am America
Ferrera in *Ugly*
Betty, a Teflon face
they slide over;

have seen also,
at my fulcrum:
a lack
of plenty
a want
for grease;

and think of the godlike intelligence
analysts sampling our direct
messages for compliance. I pray
for no visitation
of their liberating angels,

having suffered enough paternal
-istic ransackings at the KGB hour,
looking for things amiss.

Let them glance me,
the dowdy other, over,
as I
brace
my teeth
for skins of persimmon,
with their star of permission,
to hit.

I.

December 31, 2010, Beebe, Arkansas.
5,000 birds fell from the sky, stunned
by the concussive boom of our fireworks
in countdown; the wall of light and sparks,
and successive flinches, collisions, a nuclear
fission within migrating flocks. Or perhaps
it was electromagnetic forcefields
(think *Under the Dome*), or weapons
tests by the government. Whatever it was,
we are the doomsday of birds.

II.

On the traintracks of cities, a new evolution,
genes squirm out of the way.
Out of our microplastics,
rodenticides, and the leprous fingers
of our glass spires:
the lengthened beak,
the velcro toes, shrunken
or exploded haunts, the ability to
trick the birdfeeder—
beckon what we must do
about the poison of our fellows.

TEMPERAMENT

Vindictive auditors do not let things go.
To bring an editorial eye to conflict,
this is my own plumage:
no society finch exactly like another.
I'm sociable with criticism.
A mirror's panoramic eyes telling all,
whatever angle the quarry.

Do I seem a chimera,
so many serial
reinventions,
moldings half-complete,
each zone an era of toil?

I need a cowl for things past
but if I flock with gregarious birds,
I may pass unseen.

I have been denied
a small tree I can watch grow,
waiting for me at the corner
of an apparitional knoll,
the ground a grassy wave
from the house valley, the farmed heaps
of cocoyam and maize above, and the two-lane
road beyond, on an avenue of
identical government quarters.
But even that house, was not mine.

What did I know of that medicinal hill?
Of that soup we, like free-range birds,
were the meat of? I knew the tobacco for snakes;
a ground star for skin; mint seasons of efirin;
choirs of aloe, lapalapa, water and bitter leaf;
snails and *Costus Spectabilis*,
surviving the hooves of coat-arm horses.
Before the herbary becomes ash,
it is a burn paste
soothing itself before others.

Owambe.
Look, we are a pain the poultice
of Rice and Stew Very Plenty
can salve. Say if you can attend.

The swarming lace is clotting with sunlight
over mating anxieties; feet rhythm in question
toward the lattice upon the pit,
the hoarse will, the stirrups of debt.

But we must remember ourselves as we could be:
come to our party.
And by the food we are healed,
so why not dance?

II

Each one a furnace,
each chest a coral of embers.
Who lit the match?
Do you see why we could fear them?
Unapproachable light, unapproachably light book.
From the first insult of glare, and smell, and umbilical arrest,
　　the refrain—*what is it?*
We couldn't have known to choose sentience,
this oxygen chamber locked from outside,
tennis-court bronchials straining to unfurl,
Fibonacci screams recurring within.
Irrupting, we cannot reach the aureole of solace,
but we can ask why that is.

Like the mice of my childhood, blowing to soothe heels they nibbled on
with white chainsaw teeth, this mood settles like 40 stories of smog,
floating before the building of carbon climbs my breath, the hand
at my chest clutching for purchase crushed, too, thoughts of escape
    squirming
in the Brownian chamber. Give me a winch poem to unspool the
    infinite turban
of brain fog; a turbine poem to ventilate those trees in my lung forest,
the ones with elastic bands of sap garroting their craning necks; I
    want a crane poem to
deconstruct the sarcophagus-heavy helmet, and corset, the luminescent
    poster-sun on the wall;
a wrecking ball poem I can hide inside—a knuckle duster
that breaks the warden's eye-socket, enjambs the signet finger in a door;
a sock poem with pennies for the kidneys of this alley—I want this
    depression pissing blood
after hits to the side; I want renal stone poems that never let go of
    corridors,
stabbing from within with boot knives; a heel poem to withstand jeers
    and be foul,
fight dirty against the adulation of sadness; and take a windlass to its
    intestines;
I am advocating violence, a hand to wrench the lead apron
from the gonads of this thing, allow it to die like the rest of us,
but not before we all get a glimpse of sun.

In the weeks after Saro-Wiwa and others of the Ogoni Nine were
hanged by Abacha and Royal Dutch Shell, the hush was heavy, as
can happen when a sample of the country is hanged. They, their
noses specifically, had been made a bugle, an alarm of order. You
imagined yourself levitating above ground for finding your pain
unbearable; eyes yolking over cheek bones from straining against
ropes around, the sand-filled drum behind, spectators on the
beach and the drafts copper bullets have let into your chest; or
ordered down by the Military Administrator's men, disposed of in
a field. Knowing the parcel that made express mail of Dele Giwa's
handsome pieces, and Kudirat's Swiss-cheesed car, it was not
difficult to choose quiet, to risk only allegory if one felt brave. As
if obeying the inappropriate graffito of my school: "Ken Saro-
Wiwa Zone. No Hanging Around, Pls.," we shuffled along, back
to the penumbras of silence round our hurricane lanterns, their
sooty chimneys the apex, the cloud of carbon above dissident
prayers. Yes, we prayed for him to die, our circumspect pleas a
temperature only the tyrannized know. Mouthpieces of Network
News inflated his hubris, our rage, nightly. Juntas made trumpets,
wheezing whistles, of our nooses, the alarm exhaled, exploding
into street parties when finally, he was killed for us.

The only way to have separated my self
from evils committed in my name
was to have denounced them. Loudly.

the mouth, open a lot as a child,
the family strove to close.

There was perhaps some internal wonder
always fighting its way out;

their perpetual worry about closed mouths—
around elders, when chewing, or dead—

of doors ajar; a flick of someone's finger
always near, when I forgot. I kept distance

on learning to measure hand spans
by sight, cubits from my cheek, velocity

of impact: the physics
of autarchic nests.

All I needed was money.
That'd show them.

But there was the aerophagia: I had had my mouth
open long enough to eat   more of the world than most.

And in time I knew to ask—*What's wrong with me?*
And at last I knew to answer—*Nothing.*

Everything I've said is true and necessary
and beautiful, and I am essential.

And I'll have nothing more to say when I die,
but my mouth will be open.

Begin here.
I'll need brutal strength.

Here's to the illness keeping me through the night.
I hear that if I take up, from now, writing on toilet paper
in diarrheal
      spurts—
secrets that will keep me
lighted in jail,
learn: to ink walls with blood,

the convenance of mnemonic
home-brew tattoos,

the man might not die
in me. Prisoner prophets: Wole, Martin,
Kenule, gird me, prepare me.
Irina Ratushinskaya's poem books: match-stakes for the soap,
burned to the mind, evidence given to a bathroom's
bunghole, comfort me. Look,
Zheng Chaolin and Hu Feng also shanked poems,
in hundreds, onto their brains.

I want prison too,
were prison a pill to brave.
I'd take that tonic, vindication in a box,
coward's initiation into the far-flung *Arkhipelág* of conscience.
Gift me then, with shackles,
but give me a pen.

I will beg this poem, no one else, for food for my family to eat.
Then I will fold it, and put it in my pocket.

If you stop
long enough
in the zebra-crossing of Fifth & Liberty in Pittsburgh
and look up
into the morning red light,
under the green hood, a siskin's plaintive protest
counts seconds
and the steps of harried crossers
streaming around.
I let her cry reel me forward,
Moses me on a black-and-white land
parting the buffalo grass hunched in
mid-lunge, to emerge beyond,
tunneled over into
another calm.

Let us pray in this valley,
in shade of the spent stacks,
amidst the night's cardboard nests
and the cool of seven a.m.;
let us be shorn for a moment
in this corridor as quiet blowtube,
oblique sun at one end, office on the other;
let delirious bobbleheads
pause in stasis awhile,
on their journey through
into purgatory.

Our fathers had tribal
fault lines, the ones we stepped around,
carved on their cheeks.
We listened for clues—
the moon a crescent colony of egrets,
their report opening the night for
the efflorescence of insect forges,
the camera flash of lightning seeing
the things we did before the rain.
We cannot stay in this place.

Sokugo is the wandering sickness.
Six incontinents shedding itchy children into oceans,
who wade across, wait in line,
and stamp into elsewhere.
Flatfeet are restless
When the grass is fire
We cannot stay in this place.

Every land we leave is Mars-maroon.
We ax the roots of trees
we cannot climb
for a raft again.
If you wonder how our
kindling is still an armada,
we hid bamboo songs in the stacks
of brick leaving the city.
We cannot stay in this place.

Forwarding addresses have not received us,
The old mailbox cancelled.
We build a green home on the interstate
(let them drive around this obscurity)
but excavators are at the door.
Because what you want must want you, too,
We cannot stay, in this place.

Occasionally constellations wink open above our heads.
Under Vulpecula, what is our obligation to neighbor birds
when their brains break
in fox mandibles?

Someone at this bus stop
is having his worst day, or best.
They'll tell him tomorrow
he won't be home tonight.
Shall we touch his shoulder, or run?
Shall we cordon him in embrace
till search parties arrive?
Is the only right thing
to join him in this blender of dance?
No one will say everyone is unsound.

And why don't more of us party
like this, windswept by Bluetooth speakers,
strobelit by phones?
Everything is blood, anyway,
but what is our obligation
when there's a plucking again?

When I learned to read the dice of ardor,
I began to follow the other imaginary lines
like the homing animals do: my augury weak
but showing me the compass sense of redpolls
that peck at earth's magnetic field, each point afire,
reading the Odù Ifá of stars and riding the sun's
position in long-exposure whorls.

I considered tasseomancy to divide infinitude—
my many coffees had to mean something. The opposite
of divination was ignorance, so I joined the congress
of seers dripping wax in water, boiling donkey heads,
reading their dinner and aquifers. I practiced Euclidian
elicitation; Socratic methodology; double-edge bibliomancy.
I considered Fāl-gūsh, that lurking beneath dark eaves

for the dropping of answers. I studied, and trusted,
the arrangements of my gut. I allowed meteorologists
their isobars, criminologists their prints. I let the iron
shavings in my blood show the lines beneath everything:
fault-line portents, seismic lines tipping teacup shorelines
over, the gravity of my wrinkling face.
Not wasting my sacrifice, I scried my remains.

It all began with the body, I find, the cradle
I was hatched in, crucible I was shelled and ground in,
the floor I was spread upon, the pestles that conquered
my resistance. I want to read my splay,
my squirm under the tiger-striping whip, for clues.
I'd been ambered in the house where I came of age
and I have followed the lines to break myself out.

DERMATOSIS PAPULOSA NIGRA

At a certain age, I began to sprout
pangolin scales, and an ant swarm
beneath the orbit, you know, faceplate,
adaptation to ultraviolence, a radiation of my own—
spines and discs, spears and shields,
the whole body as armour for the eye—
amulet, incantation, cowry coat,
cower to fend from loss of sight,
from galactic lances, a whole body
as word, ward for the eye, prophylaxis,
pills as manhole covers above
the vitreous space of eggs,
their nuclear stars, the shelled brain
growing into corrugated shield,
a dress of rollup doors for
my final evolution: rock, in the fire,
not burnt.

BELIEVE THE MERFOLK / PEARL-HEADED
for Wangechi Mutu

You had believed us to be beautiful
but nguva, the manatees of subsea trenches have
no light no eye no need for iridescence:
do have pressured skin, ladle mouths,
strainer teeth for plankton.
And when the weight of water is good,
it is amniotic
and we grow flat.

Merpeople are beached off Indian Oceans when
fishers disbelieve their eyes, when
seashelves exile us and we must
grow sight wrest fins into hands leave home when
the things we want
invite us to air-hunger but
we repartee in migrant schools,
shoal elsewhere to trident-stabs when we emerge,
burned dinghies melted on
grasping arms.

We have tunneled from under the bioluminous lakes,
our skirts occurring for air again in turquoise war-
ning, as torches guarding the shoreline see us fulfill ourselves:
the fearsome tide, the phosphor glow,   the arcane coral,
the carnivore stories swapped by twilight.
Believe in us, or do not,
here we are.

CARDUELIS: BEHAVIORAL INTERVIEW

Describe your interaction with a difficult
headwind, your rise against it: pinions
the heart valves of a reluctant death,
trashing in a drown of blue blood;

your method of staying aloft,
palm of a heavy sky on your brow, how you swam,
cycled, climbed drafts that were flash flood,
then viscid wax, avalanche then mudslide.

Tell me: of the time you had to rely
on intermittent, and maneuvering flight;
a time you faced conflict while
stargazing, twirling, flying poor,

a contradiction of plumbing bobs.
Describe that time. You struggled to build
a burrow—to vole, through tracts of sky,
a tunnel that wouldn't collapse.

Discuss your praxis, memory movement. If earth
were a pond with landmarks, lily pads
that brought you here, for the way back, how did you bank,
twirling bags of drag in locomotion?

What was memorable on your trips
from one cage stack, and cul-de-sac, to the next?
We all make mistakes we wish we could take back.
Having leached your bony calcium for eggshells,

do you wish you'd held some back?
Describe a time you showed leadership
of your flagging apparatus, motivating your team
of body and will into volant assembly.

You saw a problem, you took the initiative
to consist, cohere.
Tell me about a time you failed.
What lessons did you learn

about the transactional conviviality
of captive flocks? How did you learn
not to mistake the dancing, the undulating flight
of your flock for a party, a family?

They parted for predators and you fell,
in ornithopter rain, to earth.
In a time you were under a lot of pressure,
tell me about a time you set a goal for yourself,

how you achieved it.
What I really want you to tell me is
how you grew your red mask once more,
renewing your fight against the fall.

The feet of this monumental sadness, artists tell me,
are the hardest to draw, toenails growing
fantastically long as I sketch.
Must I consign glimpses
of unsightly hope to rolled carpets,
pouring them, squirming,
into concrete walls of reparations
and retributions, justifications
of melancholia?

Humanity stumbles evermore
on rebellions of the circumstantial puppets
burning again the house that rage built,
who never needed to cohere,
but chose to.

They wait for me in the morning
amidst the cinders beneath my eyes.

They've stepped beside the rills,
abseiling round my crows' feet.

My irises are blast doors,
the metronome gears inside wobbly.

My cornea is tempered glass,
my sclerae matador-red.

but still, descended on climbing ropes and grapnels,
here they are.

I smile as they crowd toward me.
Hi there.

You have a genetic job to do, I know—
you need to unmake this temple.

You're early, but to be safe I've already
quartered my mind away.

When conditions are right for people,
some are known to sprout.

CHLORIS

I.

Pica in Picasso's MoMA.
To reclaim some Africa with the mouth,
or a taste of theatre:

horns holding
eighteen other strokes
in a low that stamped the ground,
hummed atelier glass
and escaped for the street,
commas shrouded upon
the stampeded dead of Turin.

II.

They bring the little children unto him.

He sketches two chambers
between heart-lung machines,
bisects them with a stroke—
a rerouted river,
a Picasso Heart.
It beats, see?
Look from under.

Some words induce a sensation of falling,
burrs to catch your breath; some
phrases expand your gums and jaws
with things held back. Prognathia,
some call that
flailing of your facial arms.
But who knows how words mix with
chemical anguish into the homemade bombs
people put in their children,
explosions stacked
like neutron seeds
into the sky?

Superstitious, they once told me
never to answer my name if loudly called,
and I didn't know who. Could be spirits,
stealing my life away. Still,
I incline my ear to words
that send back the boxcar, scoop
more birds from the mine. Some
words expunge themselves
from you like a silent room
vacuuming your ears. If

our language half-dies
in our hands like all languages must, a
neo logos, not in dictionaries,
can begin us again.
Not knowing what waits beyond I
name this my question and
answer.

FIELD DRESSING / CROSSBILL

Word problem: if, after papal bulls gave us to perpetual servitude,
we were an animal on its side, and Europe approached from Berlin

with wadded treaties for the hilts of crosscutting Gatlings, to wound
belief in the solemn word from the breast, through coastal

incisions; and from the belly, coils of bronzed trade routes, ivory
of our gentle harvest, the embrace of strangers, the ideograms

of societies; giving concussion, hatred of the vernacular, gunships,
for awakening, in how many generations did protectorates lose

their memory, and language,
their once, and future, civilization?

III

HOUSE

I am fortunate to be aware of my vivisection
by the invisible hand of the market.

Beyond, through the library's plate glass,
a mimesis of gulls as crop dusters over the bay.

For some reason they do not know, finches have decided
to overtake the world, but first, the surgery, the unremovable tag.

In family skirmishes that have taken over the world, children
have always served as human shields. We can all agree
that this should stop. But children,
you've been given a job to do. Prevent your mother's divorce,
your father's suicide; compound the grain you've been given,
and give it back again. You're the answer: granary in the winter.
There will be no solitary deaths.

(You can't tell bruises from my painted plumes and if you can,
I'd say it was deliberate.)

There is no fear (in love) / spare the rod (and spoil, soil, *the child)=*
I only shattered, smelted you because I love you + x^2
Solve this differential equation.

(Developed from the negative, I worked to be apposite in every way.)

The solution is the flinch of adult children on the phone,
still bowing slightly to the father in the east.
Hello.
I know. We haven't spoken in a while.

We haven't spoken in a while but this can work
in either of two ways when you read, imbibe this:
    1. The Pat Conroy: the apology, the work,
        as long as you're able, to make it right; the laugh
        at your caricatured self, signing books as well at the readings;
    2. Ragnarök:

the classical end of entropy.
The possible beginning: atomic raft,
oil slick of space-time stretching out, forever,
the codex of our inevitability, the necklace of causality,
blown up. Everything we would be,
we somehow already were,
and in the cumulative upheaval,
of my life, everything somehow
remained the same.

Things could not remain the same.
I see why Durden needed to destroy
at least his own terrarium, but ideally,
others too, breaking the covalent
axle of the wheel
in a triumph of Thanatos over Eros.

If the simulation of pain has a kill switch,
we have tried to find it, we have bewailed its hiding,
we have rejoiced in its existence, we have shivered at its knowledge.

Knowledge in the hard case of my skull,
an expansile notion within.
The skull does not give in to that pressure,
the brain does, downward, into the too-small
base of the skull, and the cone of death. Or perhaps
this knowledge will dissect my chest first
as I bleed out fast if I bear down hard enough.

Here is the final, and only meaning:
entropy has no reason.
Entropy resolves towards a reason,
in this case the question I always return to:
What I would have been
had I not been so afraid of you.

I'm scared of Mengele's deuteragonist:
the watercolorist of Auschwitz. Why
and more importantly, how could he
(it would have been a man) do it?

Procurers of serial spectacles for
killer court appearances; installers
of tripods that held nefarious cameras,
turn the lens back on them. J.T. Zealy

denuding Renty and Delia,
for Agassiz daguerreotypes. The electrician
of George Stinney's brief reign on the chair
at 14. The mirage, the altamirage,

adjusting the focal length of historical view.
Fear us too, the rest at rest. As
others are ploughed into the field,
we kneel beside, sorry this is all happening.

Sorry this is happening, but this is a summons:
break me into offices of hope.

They'll one day ask why we put up with it,
but let us first into offices of hope.

Where's a ten-printer to background-check me,
drug-test me in offices of dope?

When will I be found by Applicant Tracking Systems,
to nominate me for offices of hope?

After the financial crisis, doors were unkind
to stampeders toward offices of hope.

There's a railroad of windowwashers, their necktie pulleys
pinstripe offices with rope.

The world, see, is uncivil outside. Cardinals stab
with ulnas in the offices of popes.

Amity Street is strewn with rifled wallets,
antediluvian rains wash offices downslope.

I didn't wipe the blood of that crush outside, I must warn,
I won't be clean for offices of hope.

Jobs can be awful, but we need jobs.
We thank the masters of offices of hope.

Show your belly and bow deep,
performance is assessed in offices of hope.

Stress ulcers are my pyrophagia,
we burp mandalas in offices of hope.

At workbenches, chocolate cannot calm you
when you're poor in these offices. The dop-

amine, the endorphins,
will fail you at orifices of hope.

The year planners of the laid-off
will taunt those left with the awfulness of hope.

Big Corporate will end life support—
harvest organs under auspices of hope.

We'll be martial still when we come home,
bringing friendly fire from offices of hope;

trigger fingers left clawed; crosseyed
from gunsights, and gunfights in offices of trope.

Step back from my stalactite of sweat
my stick is needlessly sharp from offices of hope.

Restroom/bathroom/washroom: names chronicle our
migrancy—through nations for their offices of hope.

I, too, wanted to charge corporations by the hour,
and change the locks to offices of hope,

to be good enough; a cordon bleu Tolu,
redeeming all the promises of hope.

Park as window in the concrete, a redeeming commandment, a
sacrament of pilgrimage. If I sit here, will olfactory memories fall
from the cribriform roof of my nose, will the smog, head cold of
anhedonia? The whole decade of contrasts hoarded there; the
grandchild-shaped bottle corks that do not forget cousins; the
Manchester papers tumbling onto a morning under the almond tree,
dysphoria stabbing me in the shin when I wasn't looking? I need a
country to recycle me, and all of it; bonus points for refineries of
crude grieving. Crowded by exile, there remains the ghost, prompted
by groves, of the pristine. Ship me back something to believe.

Even ship-dredged canals
hid the carbon dome upon
gardens undisturbed.

Canopy undisturbed,
I do not know how to descend this tree
if I'll be alone when I arrive.

Far from the photographer I was in the rain,
striving to capture friends under an umbrella
on bookshop steps, disobeying love;

far from the other country that ate its children,
I surrender to repair. There's a ripple of a cure afar.
I'm fortunate to be aware of my vivisection.

Yard / African Silverbill (*Lonchura cantans*): "What did I know" riffs off Robert Hayden's "Those Winter Sundays."

Bill-sweep (American Goldfinch, *Spinus tristis*): Written after Nina Simone's "Feeling Good," and samples some of its imagery.

Atticus Finch: References the eponymous character in Harper Lee's novels *To Kill a Mockingbird* and *Go Set a Watchman*.

Waxbill / The Death of David Oluwale (Black-rumped Waxbill, *Estrilda troglodytes*): David Oluwale was a Nigerian immigrant who faced police harassment and abuse for much of the 20 years he spent in the UK, after arriving as a stowaway. Of note was his persecution by Geoffrey Ellerker and Sergeant Kenneth Kitching of the Leeds police, who were tried for his killing (and controversially acquitted). The "Least Concern" quote is from the Wikipedia entry for Least Concern Species, available at https://en.wikipedia.org/wiki/Least-concern_species (last accessed May 14, 2019).

The epigraph is from the Wikipedia entry on the Death of David Oluwale, available at https://en.wikipedia.org/wiki/Death_of_David_Oluwale (last accessed May 14, 2019).

Brimstone (Brimstone Canary, *Crithagra sulphuratus*): I. Mass bird deaths source: https://news.nationalgeographic.com/news/2011/01/110106-birds-falling-from-sky-bird-deaths-arkansas-science/ https://mysteriousuniverse.org/2018/02/hundreds-of-birds-mysteriously-fall-from-sky-in-utah-and-rome/
II. Evolution of urban animals sources: https://www.cbc.ca/news/technology/urban-evolution-cities-1.4383733

https://www.theatlantic.com/science/archive/2018/01/urban-birds-are-evolving-to-be-fed/551120/
https://news.nationalgeographic.com/2016/04/160418-animals-urban-cities-wildlife-science-coyotes/

Bucanetes (*Bucanetes githagineus*): trumpeter, from the ancient Greek.

Carduelis: Behavioral Interview (*Carduelis carduelis*): Italicized portions quoted or modified from Zhang, L. (2015, April 21). 30 Behavioral Interview Questions to Prep For. Retrieved June 8, 2019, from https://www.themuse.com/advice/30-behavioral-interview-questions-you-should-be-ready-to-answer Additional reference made to Tobalske, BW. Biomechanics of bird flight. *Journal of Experimental Biology* 2007 210: 3135-3146; doi: 10.1242/jeb.000273; The Birdcare Company. (n.d.). Neck twisting and poor flying. Retrieved June 9, 2019, from https://birdcareco-shop.com/neck-twisting-and-poor-flying/; and Ellison, G. (2018, June 13). Nature Journal: Goldfinches soar with the grace of ballet dancers. Retrieved June 9, 2019, from https://www.citizen-times.com/story/life/2018/06/13/nature-journal-goldfinches-soar-grace-ballet-dancers/676830002/

Chestnut and White Munia (*Lonchura maja*): Reference: *The Guide to Owning a Finch*, by Rod Fischer, (c) 2002 by T.F.H Publications, Inc.

Chloris (*Chloris ambigua*): A Picasso Heart is an expression I first encountered when I read the story of Ethan Chandra, who, as a result of heterotaxy needed extensive cardiac reconstructive surgery. His mother called his new heart, post-operatively, a "Picasso Heart." Story here: https://blogs.mprnews.org/newscut/2017/06/mom-of-boy-with-rare-heart-condition-puts-human-face-on-health-debate/

Disorganized Attachment (Common Cactus Finch, *Geospiza scandens*): The common cactus finch is a Galápagos finch that shows extreme affinity for the prickly pear cactus.

Elementary Divination (Common Redpoll, *Acanthis flammea*): Written after Adam Zagajewski's poem, "Mysticism for Beginners," from a prompt I am grateful to Michael Edwards for. Common redpolls occasionally migrate in massive numbers, in southward irruptions when their food supplies dwindle.

Eophonia (*Eophonia migratoria*): from the classical Greek for dawn+cry.

Euphonia (*Euphonia musica*): The Euphonia (also a kind of finch, not to be confused with the *eophonia*, another finch), was a "speaking" automaton completed and exhibited by Joseph Faber in 1845, but so named by P.T. Barnum.

Galápagos (Galápagos Finch, subfamily *Geospizinae*): This poem was inspired by (with text in italics quoted directly from) Charles Darwin's *A Naturalist's Voyage Round the World*, originally published in 1860, and made available by Project Gutenberg. http://www.gutenberg.org/files/3704/3704-h/3704-h.htm Each island of the Galápagos archipelago had its own distinctive species of finch, depending on what kinds of seeds were available to them. This has fascinated evolutionary biologists for over a century, and has been extensively studied.

Golden Crowned Bishop (*Euplectes afer*): The story of Renty, Delia, and others can be found here: https://www.usatoday.com/story/news/nation/2019/03/21/harvard-slavery-lawsuit-who-renty-american-slave-photos/3232806002/

Portrait of the artist as Gouldian chick in freefall from the nest
(Gouldian Finch, *Chloebia gouldiae*). Adult Gouldian finches,
especially those who are new parents, have often been observed
tossing their young, frequently leading to the non-survival of
these chicks.

Green Singing (Green Singing Finch, *Crithagra mozambica*): is for
Teju Cole. Sokugo: wandering sickness, was introduced to the author
in *Burning Grass*, a 1962 novel by Cyprian Ekwensi in which the
protagonist is afflicted with a wandering spell.

Hawfinch (*Coccothraustes coccothraustes*): the hawfinch is characterized
by its unobtrusive cry.

House (House Finch, *Haemorhous mexicanus*): Italicized portion was
modified from a quote attributed to the ornithologist Alexander
Badyaev in *The Atlantic* article "Urban Bird Feeders Are Changing
the Course of Evolution," by Emily Voigt. https://www.theatlantic
.com/science/archive/2018/01/urban-birds-are-evolving-to-be
-fed/551120/

Nonpareil (Nonpareil Finch, *Erythrura prasina*): Sources: http://
blogs.thatpetplace.com/thatbirdblog/2013/02/28/breeding-and
-keeping-the-nonpareil-finch-or-pin-tailed-parrot-finch/#.XNsTiy
-ZORt, https://www.cnn.com/style/article/radium-girls
-radioactive-paint/index.html, https://www.nprillinois.org/post
/radium-girls-illinois-tragedy#stream/o (all last accessed May 14,
2019); *The Guide to Owning a Finch*, by Rod Fischer, (c) 2002 by
T.F.H Publications, Inc.
   "The Society" is from the actual "Society of the Living Dead,"
former "Radium Girls" who had been poisoned while working at
radium paint companies, suffering catastrophic injuries. "Undark"

was the trade name for Radium-based paint as marketed by the US Radium Corporation in the early 20th century.

'Ō'ū (*Psittirostra psittacea*): The 'Ō'ū bird is endemic to the Hawaiian islands, and is conjectured to be extinct. The URLs this found poem were constructed from are for webpages about the bird. *Ou*, a different word, is French for *or*.

Painted Bunting (*Passerina ciris*): "There will be no solitary deaths," and indeed this entire collection, was inspired by this passage in the incomparable Dionne Brand's book, *Ossuaries*: "*who will see the bedraggled gawping doorways, / the solitary deaths of finches that winters strand.*" Once I saw those finches, I began to see them everywhere.

Pyrrhula (*Pyrrhula pyrrhula*): flame-colored, in Latin.

Premonitions (Purple Finch, *Haemorhous purpureus*): The purple finch, common in urban areas, is one of the bird species most susceptible to window strikes https://bioone.org/journals/The-Condor/volume-116/issue-1/CONDOR-13-090.1/Birdbuilding-collisions-in-the-United-States--Estimates-of-annual/10.1650/CONDOR-13-090.1 .full#i0010-5422-116-1-8-t01. Taller buildings account for the majority of these bird deaths: https://www.washingtonpost.com/national /health-science/stop-blaming-cats-as-many-as-988-million-birds-die -annually-in-window-collisions/2014/02/03/9837fe80-8866-11e3 -916e-e01534b1e132_story.html?utm_term=.7b35d792ea45.

Red-browed (Red-browed Finch, *Neochmia temporalis*): is a foraging finch that nests in shrubs.

Rent-Seeking / Shaft-tail (Shaft-tail Finch, *Poephila acuticauda*): "It is not sport . . ." is a nod to Yusef Komunyakaa's "Ode to a Drum."

Urvogel (family *Archaeopterygidae*): better known as Archaeopteryx, was a dinosaur ancestor of birds, that had features of both birds and dinosaurs.

Zebra (Zebra Finch, *Taeniopygia guttata*): Italicized portion is from *The Guide to Owning a Finch*, by Rod Fischer, (c) 2002 by T.F.H Publications, Inc.

Others:

Atlantic Canary *(Serinus canaria)*
Black-bellied Firefinch *(Lagonosticta rara)*
Black-headed Finch *(Spizixos semitorques)*
Black-hooded Sierra-Finch *(Phrygilus atriceps)*
Brambling *(Fringilla montifringilla)*
Bronze Mannikin *(Spermestes cucullata)*
Canary *(Serinus canaria forma domestica)*
Common Waxbill *(Estrilda astrild)*
Cordonbleu *(Uraeginthus angolensis)*
Crossbill (genus *Loxia)*
Cutthroat Finch *(Amadina fasciata)*
Double-barred Finch *(Stizoptera bichenovii)*
Grosbeak *(Pinicola enucleator)*
Masked Grassfinch *(Poephila personata)*
Orange Weaver *(Ploceus aurantius)*
Pearl-headed Mannikin *(Lonchura griseicapilla)*
Protea Canary *(Serinus leucopterus)*
Purple Grenadier *(Uraeginthus ianthinogaster)*
Rice Bird *(Lonchura oryzivora)*
Siskin *(Spinus pinus)*
Society Finch *(Lonchura striata domestica)*
Spectacled Finch *(Callacanthis burtoni)*
Spice Finch *(Lonchura punctulata)*
Weaver Finch (family *Ploceidae)*
West African Seedeater *(Crithagra canicapilla)*

ACKNOWLEDGMENTS

"Carduelis: Behavioral Interview": First appeared in *Canadian Literature*.

"Chestnut and White Munia": First appeared in the *Kalahari Review*, as "Coherence."

"Field Dressing / Crossbill": First appeared in *The Windsor Review*.

"Green Singing Finch": First appeared in *Dappled Things*, as "Sokugo."

"Orange Weaver": First appeared in the *Canadian Medical Association Journal*.

"Painted Bunting": First appeared in *THIS Magazine*.

"Rice Bird": First appeared in *The Kalahari Review*, as "What Did the Drum Say?"

"Siskin": First appeared in *Dappled Things*, as "sparrow.eye.storm."

"The Child's Other / Spice Finch": First appeared in *Harvard Divinity Bulletin*. Reproduced with permission.

"Weaver Finch": First appeared in *Klorofyl*, as "Attrition."

This book would not exist without the vision, as well as literary and editorial sublimity, of Dionne Brand. I am grateful for the grace with which she received 20-odd finch poems, saw the book they could be before I could imagine it, and in what still feels like a dream sequence, helped shape it as it emerged while pushing me beyond what I thought possible of myself. Working with Professor Brand has been the greatest privilege of my literary career.

I am thankful for the team at McClelland & Stewart for the care with which they handled this book and produced it. I am incredibly indebted to Kelly Joseph for the clarity, effectiveness, perceptiveness, generosity, and humour with which she helped me navigate the publication process over an almost three-year period. I am grateful for Soraya Gallant's exceptional work on the manuscript as it went into design. I am honoured by Kate Sinclair's beautiful book design, and the stunning cover vortext; Blossom Thom's incisive copyediting; for Kimberlee Kemp, M&S managing editor; Kim Kandravy, M&S production coordinator, and for other M&S team members I have not named. I am also thankful to Jared Bland for advocating for this book, and publishing it, and remain extremely grateful for Canisia Lubrin's years-long guidance and friendship.

To my friends, and family, who keep me moored in a swirling world—Olatunde Asagba, Babajide Adeyefa, Aidan Chafe, Shazia Hafiz Ramji (who initially recommended *Ossuaries* to me), Caroline, Frances, Zoe—my eternal thanks.

TOLU OLORUNTOBA lived in Nigeria and the United States before settling in the metro area of Coast Salish lands known as Vancouver with his family. He spent his early career as a primary care physician, and currently manages virtual health projects with organizations in British Columbia. His poetry has been nominated for the Pushcart Prize, while his debut chapbook, *Manubrium*, was a bpNichol Chapbook Award finalist. *The Junta of Happenstance*, his first full-length collection, was the winner of the 2021 Governor General's Literary Award for English Language Poetry.